ECOUTEZ BIEN 1

Junior Certificate
Listening Comprehension Tests
SECOND EDITION REVISED
Student's Book

Joseph Dunne M.A., H.D.E.

FOLENS

Preface

Ecoutez Bien 1 provides students with suitable and adequate aural practice for the Junior Certificate Examination – where the Listening Comprehension section accounts for the largest proportion of the marks (140 out of 320).

Ecoutez Bien 1 consists of four elements:

* A Student's Book, containing the questions
* A Teacher's Tapescript
* Two audio cassette tapes
* Two CDs (provided with the Student's Book)

The cassettes and the CDs contain all the recorded material.

Great care has been taken to ensure that the material has been maintained at a level which would be realistic for Junior Certificate students.

A large number of native French speakers (adults and teenagers) have been used in the studio recordings to add variety and authenticity to the material.

Joseph Dunne
2004

Editor
Margaret Burns

Design and Layout
Paula Byrne

ISBN 978-1-84131-649-9

SET ISBN 978-1-84131-848-6

© 2004 Joseph Dunne

Folens Publishers, Hibernian Industrial Estate, Greenhills Road, Tallaght Dublin 24.

Table des matières

1. Je me présente

A French boy tells us lots of interesting things about himself.

1. What age is Antoine? ....

2. What is the date of his birthday? ....

3. What colour are his eyes? ....

4. What colour is his hair? ....

5. He has three pastimes. What are they?

   (i) ....

   (ii) ....

   (iii) ....

6. What age is his brother, Rémi? ....

★ ★ ★

7. Where do Antoine and Rémi get information about the fish they keep?

   ....

8. What two colours of fish does Antoine prefer?

   (i) ....

   (ii) ....

★ ★ ★

9. How often does Antoine change the water in the aquarium?

   ....

10. What job would he like to have later in life?

   ....

2. Une jeune fille se présente

Cédrine gives us many details about herself.

1. What age is Cédrine?..

2. What is the date of her birthday? ....

3. She says that she is optimistic, very friendly, and she loves to travel.

   True ☐   False ☐

4. What colour is her hair?..

5. What colour are her eyes? ....

★ ★ ★

6. In which French city does Cédrine live? ....

7. What age is her brother, Alain?..

8. Alain has three interests. What are they?

   (i)...

   (ii)..

   (iii)...

9. What is her father's job?...

10. What is her mother's job? ....

11. Which two foreign languages does her mother speak?

    (i)...   (ii)...

★ ★ ★

12. What job would Cédrine like to have later in life?

    ....

13. Which two languages is she studying in school?

    (i)...   (ii)...

14. What does she intend to do next July?

    ....

3. Les vacances

Three young people describe their holidays.

1. Marie-Claire

1. When did Marie-Claire go to the *colonie de vacances*?

   ....

2. Write down one aspect of the *colonie de vacances* that she enjoyed.

   ....

3. Tick the activities that she mentions:

   Playing tennis ☐   Mountain-biking ☐

   Playing volleyball ☐   Horse-riding ☐

   Canoeing ☐   Rock-climbing ☐

4. What does she hope to do next year?

   ....

★   ★   ★

2. Yves

1. In which month did Yves go to this activity centre?...........................

2. Why did he go there? ....

3. Which two manual activities did he enjoy?

   (i)...

   (ii)..

4. Yves loved the treasure hunt but he never managed to find any treasure.

   True ☐   False ☐

★   ★   ★

3. Jacqueline

1. When will Jacqueline go to the Pyrenees with her parents? ....
   ....

2. How long will they spend there? ....

3. What will they do to pass the time? *(two details)*

   (i) ....

   (ii) ....

4. What will they have in the evenings? ....

5. They will go on excursions to see the beautiful villages.

   True ☐   False ☐

un moniteur

le canoë-kayak

le VTT

un centre aéré

une activité manuelle

la chasse au trésor

les sorties

les environs

les barbecues

4. Les passe-temps

Four young people speak of their pastimes.

1. Nicole

1. How does Nicole like to spend her free time? ....

2. On which two days does she go swimming?

    (i).......................................   (ii)...

3. For what two reasons does she like walking?

    (i)..

    (ii)..

★ ★ ★

2. Hervé

1. What is Hervé's occupation? ....

2. What does he do in the evening to relax?...

3. Which type of book does he prefer?..

★ ★ ★

3. Pauline

1. When, in particular, does Pauline like to go window-shopping?

    ....

2. Tick the items of clothing that she mentions:

Blouses		Skirts	
Socks		Hats	
Jumpers		Trousers	

3. Tick the accessories that she mentions:

A belt		A ring	
A bracelet		A scarf	
A bag		A necklace	

★   ★   ★

4. Pierre

1. At what stage in his life used Pierre like to collect things? ....

2. Tick the items that he liked to collect:

Cinema tickets		Cheese labels	
Telephone cards		Stamps	
Beer mats		Coins	

3. Where are all his collections now?..

4. Today, what does he do to amuse himself? ....

On respire l'air pur.
Je fais du lèche-vitrines.
Rien ne vaut un bon livre.

5. Projets pour un samedi soir

Young people are making plans for Saturday evening!

1. Sandrine and Roger

1. Roger can't go out because he is ill.

   True ☐   False ☐

2. Two people are coming to visit Roger's family. Who are they?

   (i)...

   (ii)..

★　★　★

2. Marie and Pierre

1. When will the party take place at Carole's house?

   ....

2. Whom is she inviting to the party?...

3. Where does Carole live? ....

★　★　★

3. Virginie and Valérie

1. What type of film is showing in the cinema?

   ....

2. Whom will they invite to come with them?...

3. Fill in the final digits of the mobile telephone number:

| 0 | 6 | 7 | 8 | 5 | 6 | _ | _ | _ | _ |

4. Fill in the details of where and when they will meet:

   Place: ....

   Time: ....

6. Au collège

Jean-Paul gives us lots of information about his school-life.

1. In which French city is the school situated? ....

2. How many subjects does Jean-Paul study? ....

3. He mentions three languages in his list of subjects.

   True ☐   False ☐

   ★   ★   ★

4. What is his favourite language in school? ....

5. For what reason is this a useful language for him? ....

6. Which subject does he not like? ....

7. He gives two reasons for not liking this subject. What are they?

   (i) ....

   (ii) ....

   ★   ★   ★

8. What size is his school? ....

9. Jean-Paul mentions four sports. What are they?

   (i) ....

   (ii) ....

   (iii) ....

   (iv) ....

10. In his school, there is a computer room and a large library.

    True ☐   False ☐

11. His parents have got his school report!
    In which two subjects did he get good marks?

    (i)...

    (ii)..

12. He got bad marks in biology and history.

    True ☐   False ☐

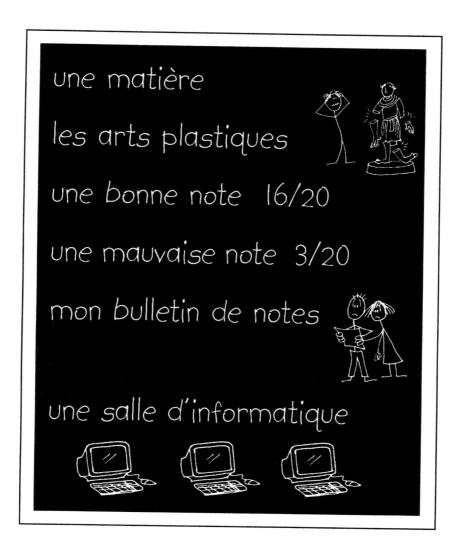

7. A la gare

You will hear three conversations about train tickets.

1. First traveller

1. Where does this person wish to go? ....

2. Does he want a single ticket or a return ticket?...

3. Fill in the details in the grid:

Departure time of train	
Arrival time	
Cost of ticket	€

★   ★   ★

2. Second traveller

1. Fill in the details in the grid:

Departure time from Lille	
Arrival time in Strasbourg	
City where she must change trains	

2. She has three hours to change trains.

True ☐   False ☐

★   ★   ★

3. Third traveller

Fill in the details in the grid:

City of departure	
City of destination	
Cost of ticket at peak times	€
Cost of ticket at normal times	€
Time of departure	
Time of arrival	

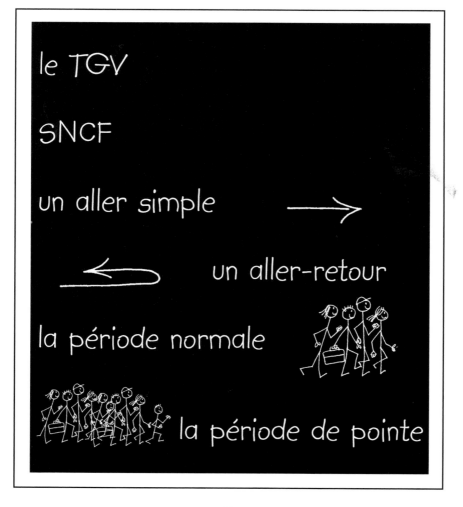

8. Si on allait manger ?

You will hear two conversations about dining in restaurants.

1. Julie and François

1. What special occasion are they celebrating? ....

2. What food item does Julie seem to not like? ....

3. Fill in the missing digits in the telephone number:

0	1	_	_	3	4	3	1	_	_

★ ★ ★

4. How many people will be in the group? ....

5. At what time should everybody be there? ....

★ ★ ★

2. Isabelle and Paul

1. Where is the new self-service restaurant situated?

....

2. How much did it cost to have chicken with one vegetable?

....

3. When were fish and chips on the menu as the special of the day?

....

4. What is today's special? ....

....

12

9. Des vacances en Irlande

Two young French people talk about their holidays in Ireland.

1. Françoise

1. When did Françoise come to Ireland? ....

2. How long was her holiday here? ....

3. What does she say about Belfast? ....

   ....

★　★　★

4. During her holiday, she particularly liked

   (a) the sweet shops
   (b) the cake shops
   (c) the clothes shops
   (d) the fish shops

   Write (a), (b), (c) or (d) in the box.　☐

★　★　★

5. What was the main difficulty that she experienced?

   ....

6. What does she like to do when she visits a country?

   (a) Learn about its history
   (b) Explore the countryside
   (c) Talk with the people
   (d) Visit the museums

   Write (a), (b), (c) or (d) in the box.　☐

★　★　★

2. Hervé

1. How long has Hervé been on holidays in Ireland?.......................................

2. When must he return to France?.......................................

3. At what time has he to be at the airport? ....

4. How many more days are left before he returns to school? ....

★   ★   ★

5. What part of Ireland did he like best?.......................................

6. In Donegal, he says that nature is wild and the winds are gentle.

    True ☐   False ☐

7. In Dublin, which one of the following does he not mention?

    (a) The vandalism
    (b) The crowds of people
    (c) The traffic
    (d) The traffic jams

    Write (a), (b), (c) or (d) in the box.   ☐

10. Les informations

You will hear three news items and a weather forecast.

1. First news item

1. When did this road accident take place? ....
2. In which French city did it occur? ....
3. What age was the boy who was killed in the accident? ....
4. The collision was between a large truck and

    (a) a motorcar

    (b) a van

    (c) a mountain-bike

    (d) a motorbike

    Write (a), (b), (c) or (d) in the box.

5. At what time of the year did this accident take place? ....
6. With whom was the boy staying? ....

★   ★   ★

2. Second news item

1. What nationality were the tourists who were killed? ....
2. On which day of the week did the storm occur? ....
3. Which part of France was most affected? ....
4. What depth of rain fell in three hours? ....

★   ★   ★

3. Third news item

1. When exactly did this helicopter crash take place? ....
2. What nationality was the pilot? ....
3. Where exactly did this crash occur? ....
4. How many people were killed? ....

★   ★   ★

15

4. Weather forecast

1. For what date is this weather forecast? ....

2. Tomorrow morning, it will be quite warm and the winds will be light.

   True ☐   False ☐

3. During the afternoon, in Normandy and Brittany there will be

   (a) showers of rain
   (b) thunder storms
   (c) snow
   (d) strong winds

   Write (a), (b), (c) or (d) in the box. ☐

4. In general, what can the people of France look forward to tomorrow?

   ....

l'ensemble
du pays

— des vents légers

— des vents modérés

— des vents forts

une averse

11. La météo

You will hear the weather forecast for four regions in France.

1. The Mediterranean region

1. What will tomorrow's weather be like in this region? ....
   ....

2. What will be noticeable in the afternoon? ....

3. Fill in the temperatures:

Morning	
Afternoon	

★   ★   ★

2. Alsace-Lorraine

1. In the morning, it will be cloudy and there will be some showers of rain.

   True ☐   False ☐

2. What will appear in the afternoon? ....

3. Fill in the temperatures:

Morning	
Afternoon	

★   ★   ★

3. Normandy

1. What is the forecast for the morning in Normandy?
   ....

2. It will be colder in the afternoon.

   True ☐   False ☐

3. What is the highest temperature that can be expected? ....

★   ★   ★

4. The Alps

1. What is the weather forecast for the morning in the Alps?

    ....

2. There will be lots of clouds.

    True ☐   False ☐

3. What kind of winds are forecast?..

4. What is the maximum temperature forecast for the valleys? ....

Les températures seront agréables

Le soleil fera son apparition

Il pleuvra demain

Pas un nuage

12. Dans les magasins

People are shopping. They visit three shops.

1. The baker's

1. What does Laurent buy? *(two details)*

    (i)...

    (ii)...

2. How much does he pay for the items?...

3. How much change does he get?...

★ ★ ★

2. The florist's

1. Why does the girl want to buy a plant?

    ....

2. Fill in the cost of each type of plant:

A plant with red flowers	€
A plant with white flowers	€

3. Which plant does she choose to buy?...

★ ★ ★

3. The supermarket

1. Which section in the supermarket is the lady looking for?

    ....

2. Where, in the supermarket, is this section situated?

    ....

3. What item does the lady want to buy?

    ....

13. Lieux de vie

Three people tell us about where they live.

1. Henri

1. Where does Henri live? ....

2. Why does Henri like living there? *(two details)*

   (i)...

   (ii)..

3. Henri and his friends amuse themselves

   (a) on their mountain–bikes
   (b) by singing ballads
   (c) by listening to music
   (d) by going walking in the woods

   Write (a), (b), (c) or (d) in the box.

   ★   ★   ★

4. What does he say is the one problem about living where he does?
   ....

5. What does he hope to have next year?

   ....

   ★   ★   ★

2. Mireille

1. Where does Mireille live?...

2. What is the advantage of living there?

   ....

3. From which century does the building date? ....

   ★   ★   ★

4. How many rooms are there in her home?

   (a) 6

   (b) 7

   (c) 8

   (d) 9

   Write (a), (b), (c) or (d) in the box.

5. From the window of her bedroom, what can she see? *(two details)*

   (i)...

   (ii)...

★   ★   ★

3. Nicole

1. On which floor of the apartment block does Nicole live?.........................

2. When, in particular, does she find it difficult to live there?

   ....

3. Why don't her parents move to a nicer home? ....

   ....

4. What, for Nicole, is the main advantage of living there?

   ....

- on fait une balade
- une HLM
- un immeuble
- un gratte-ciel
- en panne

EN PANNE

21

14. Les anniversaires

Birthdays are coming up soon! People are discussing them.

1. Céline and Pierre

1. When will it be grandmother's birthday?...

2. What age will she be? ....

★   ★   ★

3. Who are coming from Canada?...

4. Who are coming from Corsica? ....

★   ★   ★

2. Dominique and Eric

1. Fill in the missing digits in the telephone number:

0	5	_	_	6	5	1	6	_	_

2. What is the name of the girl who will be celebrating her birthday with a party?

   ....

3. Fill in the details about the party:

Day	
Date	
Time	

★   ★   ★

4. They discuss the idea of buying a combined present. How much money will each person contribute?

   ....

5. Which one of the two will look after collecting the money?

   ....

15. Mes vacances : deux jeunes parlent

Two young people tell us about their holidays.

1. Pascal

1. In which month did Pascal go on holidays? ....

2. Where did he go? ....

3. Where did he stay while there? ....

4. How long did the holiday last? ....

5. Which colour ski slopes are the most difficult? ....

6. With whom did he ski on these slopes? ....

★ ★ ★

7. What colour slopes do his mother and sister prefer? *(two details)*

    (i) ....

    (ii) ....

8. Which sport is a new one for Pascal? ....

★ ★ ★

2. Sylvie

1. How long more does Sylvie have to wait before going to the beach?

    (a) A day

    (b) A week

    (c) A fortnight

    (d) A month

    Write (a), (b), (c) or (d) in the box.

2. What has she already bought? *(three details)*

    (i) ....

    (ii) ....

    (iii) ....

3. With whom is she going on holidays? *(two details)*

    (i)...

    (ii)...

4. Tick the activities that she mentions:

Cinema		Sailing	
Disco		Boxing	
Sport		Scuba-diving	
Games		Cycling	

les pistes

les activités de l'après-ski

on sortira ensemble

un maillot de bain

la plongée sous-marine

16. Chez le coiffeur

Two people visit the hairstylist's.

1. The lady

1. For what time has Valérie Chambaud an appointment? ....

2. Where does the hairstylist ask her to sit? ....

3. What type of cut does the hairstylist recommend?

    (a) Very long

    (b) Short

    (c) Very short

    (d) Curly

    Write (a), (b), (c) or (d) in the box.

★   ★   ★

2. The young man

1. What reason does the young man give for coming to the hairstylist?

    ....

2. What style does the hairstylist recommend? *(two details)*

    (i)...

    (ii)..

3. The young man says that he will resemble

    (a) a squirrel

    (b) a hedgehog

    (c) a punk rocker

    (d) a film star

    Write (a), (b), (c) or (d) in the box.

17. Les loisirs

Three people talk to us about their pastimes.

1. Julie

1. What sport does Julie play? ....

2. On which two evenings does she play?

    (i)..

    (ii)...

3. When, particularly, does she play in tournaments?..................................

★   ★   ★

2. Patrick

1. Which musical instrument does Patrick play? ....

2. What are he and his friend looking for? ....

3. Where are they going to place advertisements?......................................

4. What CDs does he have? ....

★   ★   ★

3. Colette

1. What is Colette's pastime?..

2. When was she given a present? ....

3. She spends all her free time engaged in this pastime.

    True ☐   False ☐

★   ★   ★

4. How does she reduce the cost of her hobby?

    ....

18. Un après-midi

Plans are being made for the afternoon!

1. Stéphanie and Corinne

1. What are Stéphanie and Corinne planning to do for the afternoon?

   ....

2. What is Corinne looking for?

   (a) A hat

   (b) Shoes

   (c) A blouse

   (d) A shirt

   Write (a), (b), (c) or (d) in the box.

3. When did Corinne buy a skirt?...

4. How much did Stéphanie pay for the pullover?.................................

★   ★   ★

2. Fréderic and Alain

1. Fréderic has just got a text-message from his friend, Daniel. What does Daniel want Fréderic and Alain to do?

   ....

2. Why is Fréderic keen to accept the invitation?

   ....

3. What restriction does Fréderic's parents impose on him?

   ....

4. Alain says that he hopes to get a present from his new friend, Noel.

   True ☐   False ☐

19. Les téléphones portables

Young people are discussing their mobile phones.

1. Pierre and Marie

1. What is the first thing that Marie tells Pierre about her mobile phone?

   ....

2. Her mobile has lots of functions. Write down two of them.

   (i)...

   (ii)..

3. How much did Marie's phone cost? ....

4. Who gave her the phone? ....

★   ★   ★

2. Sophie and Marc

1. Sophie does not like the ring-tone of Marc's mobile.

   True ☐   False ☐

2. Where did Marc find his ring-tone? ....

3. What is the first thing that the website asks you to do?

   ....

4. When will Sophie try to do what Marc has done? ....

20. Présentations : un garçon et une fille

Two young people describe themselves.

1. Cédric
Fill in the details in the grid:

Age	
Date of birthday	
City	
Colour of eyes	
Colour of hair	
Mother's job	
Father's job	
Number of brothers and sisters	
Girlfriend's name	
Hobbies	(i) (ii) (iii)

★   ★   ★

2. Karima

Fill in the details in the grid:

Parents' country of origin	
Karima's age	
Brother's age	
Sister's age	
Father's job	
Mother's job	
Weekend leisure activities	(i)
	(ii)
	(iii)

21. A la gare

People are buying train tickets.

1. First traveller

1. Fill in the details in the grid:

City of departure	
Destination	*Rennes*
Type of ticket bought	
% reduction for students	%
Platform number	

★   ★   ★

2. Second traveller

1. To which French city does the lady want to go?.....................................

2. On what two days of the week do you have to change trains at Lyon?

    (i)...

    (ii)...

3. At what time does the next train leave?...

4. From which platform does it leave?..

★   ★   ★

5. What type of ticket does the lady buy?...

6. How much does the ticket cost?...

7. How much extra does she pay for a reserved seat? ....

22. L'emploi du temps au collège

Students are discussing their timetable and the subjects that they will be studying in the new school year.

1. Antoine and Carole

1. On what date of the year does this conversation take place?......................

2. What two languages is Carole studying this academic year?

    (i)...

    (ii)..

3. What two science subjects is Antoine studying?

    (i)...

    (ii)..

★ ★ ★

4. Why does Antoine like science subjects?

    ....

5. Why does he like his science teacher, Madame Moreau? *(two details)*

    (i)...

    (ii)..

★ ★ ★

2. Bernard and Sylvie

1. What aspect of school life does Bernard like?

    ....

2. What two subjects does Sylvie really like?

    (i)...

    (ii)..

3. Bernard doesn't like geography because he says that the world is much too big for him!

    True ☐   False ☐

    ★   ★   ★

4. Tick the sports that Bernard practises:

    Athletics ☐   Tennis ☐
    Basketball ☐   Football ☐
    Golf ☐   Horse-riding ☐
    Swimming ☐   Fishing ☐

23. A l'office de tourisme

1. First tourist

1. What is this man looking for? ....

2. What do the numbers represent? ....

3. On the back of the map there is a list of hotels and youth hostels.

   True ☐   False ☐

   ★　　★　　★

2. Second tourist

1. Fill in the details on the booking-form for the **Son et lumière** show:

Town	
Date	
Number of adults	
Number of children	
Price per adult	€
Price per child	€
Total cost	€
Method of payment	Cash ☐ Cheque ☐ Credit card ☐

★　　★　　★

3. Third tourist

1. In which French city is the tourist office situated? ....

2. How long does this tourist intend to spend in the region? ....

3. In which month will she come to visit the town? ....

4. What is the lady's surname?

L						

5. In which city does she live? ....

24. Les régimes alimentaires

People are discussing diets.

1. Monique and Marie

1. When did their friend, Sophie, start her diet? ....

2. Why has Sophie decided to go on a diet?

   ....

3. Tick the food items mentioned:

Fruit	☐	Cheese	☐
Vegetables	☐	Dairy products	☐
Fish	☐	Chicken	☐

4. What must Sophie drink? ....

★   ★   ★

2. Paul and Jacques

1. When did their friend, Pierre, begin his basketball training? ....

2. Why has Pierre to go on a diet? ....

3. Tick the food items mentioned:

Meat	☐	Cheese	☐
Fish	☐	Cereals	☐
Green vegetables	☐	Yogurts	☐
Pasta	☐	Fruit	☐

4. If he follows this diet, what will be the result for Pierre?

   ....

25. Les informations

You will hear three news items and a traffic report.

1. First news item

1. At what time did this accident take place? ....

2. How many young people died? ....

3. For how long had the driver his licence? ....

4. What colour was the car? ....

5. According to a witness, the driver was trying to avoid

   (a) a pedestrian

   (b) a horse

   (c) a dog

   (d) a cyclist

   Write (a), (b), (c) or (d) in the box.

★   ★   ★

2. Second news item

1. This house was destroyed

   (a) in a flood

   (b) in a fire

   (c) by lightning

   (d) by a truck crashing into it

   Write (a), (b), (c) or (d) in the box.

2. When did this occur? ....

3. How many people were injured? ....

4. What injuries did they sustain? *(two details)*

   (i) ....

   (ii) ....

★   ★   ★

3. Third news item

1. In which city does the couple live? ....

2. What generous deed have they done? ....

3. How long will the girl remain in France? ....

★   ★   ★

4. Traffic report

1. Motorists are advised to avoid the A3 because of

    (a) an accident

    (b) road works

    (c) ice

    (d) a protest

    Write (a), (b), (c) or (d) in the box.

2. Which road are they advised to take instead? ....

26. La météo

You will hear four weather forecasts ... each one for a different time of the year.

1. August

1. For which date in August is this forecast? ....

2. Fill in the details in the grid:

Two comments about the weather	(i) (ii)
Minimum temperature	
Maximum temperature	

3. What advice are you given, if you are going to the beach?

   ....

★ ★ ★

2. November

1. For which date in November is this forecast?

2. The forecast for the morning predicts

   (a) rain

   (b) strong winds

   (c) mist

   (d) fog

   Write (a), (b), (c) or (d) in the box.   ☐

3. What will the weather for the rest of the day be like? ....

   ....

4. If you are going out, what should you remember to bring? ....

★ ★ ★

3. January

1. For which date in January is this forecast?...

2. What is the forecast? *(two details)*

   (i)...

   (ii)..

★　★　★

3. On the roads, there will be a risk of

   (a) snow
   (b) black ice
   (c) floods
   (d) fog

   Write (a), (b), (c) or (d) in the box.   ☐

★　★　★

4. March

1. For which date in March is this forecast? ....

2. The winds will be light and the sky very cloudy.

   True ☐   False ☐

3. When will it rain?..

4. What advice are you given at the end? ....

27. Randonnée et pique-nique en famille

Carole describes a family picnic and a hike in the countryside.

1. At what time did the family wake up?..

2. What was the weather like? *(two details)*

    (i)...

    (ii)..

3. What did they do the previous evening?...

4. Carole's father brought

    (a) a map

    (b) a fishing–rod

    (c) a compass

    (d) a book on plants and animals

    Which one is not included?

    Write (a), (b), (c) or (d) in the box.

5. What was in the rucksack? *(two details)*

    (i)...

    (ii)..

★ ★ ★

6. Along the way, what did they find?...

7. At what time did they stop to have the picnic?......................................

8. Which one item is not included?

Ham sandwiches ⬜   Crisps ⬜

Cheese sandwiches ⬜   Cakes ⬜

Rice salad ⬜   Yogurts ⬜

9. What did they drink? *(two details)*

(i)..

(ii)...

★   ★   ★

10. How long did the family take for a siesta? ....

11. At what time did they set out again on their hike? ....

12. The family sang songs and told funny stories.

True ⬜   False ⬜

13. At what time did the family adventure end?

une petite sieste

28. Deux passe-temps

Two young people describe their contrasting pastimes.

1. Marc

1. What is Marc's favourite sport? ....

2. On what two days does he train?

    (i)..

    (ii)...

3. When does he play a match?..

4. For how many years have Marc and his two friends, Alain and Vincent, been playing together? ....

★　★　★

5. What is Marc's favourite team?..

6. What do Marc and his two friends hope to do in a month's time?

    ....

★　★　★

2. Thérèse

1. When does Thérèse have ballet lessons?..

2. How does she contact her two friends, Yvonne and Lucienne?

    ....

3. Where, in town, are the clothes shops that she prefers? ....

★　★　★

4. Tick the items that she mentions:

A dress		A hat		A blouse	
A skirt		A scarf		Socks	

5. What will she buy in the sales?...

29. Vacances dans un camping

Jean-Yves describes a family holiday spent in a fabulous French campsite.

1. How long did the family spend in the campsite? ....

2. In which French region was the campsite? ....

3. Name three of the facilities in the campsite.

    (i)...

    (ii)...

    (iii)..

4. What was really special about the toilets?

    ....

★ ★ ★

5. Which one is not included?

    (a) A grocer's

    (b) A tourist office

    (c) A baker's

    (d) A butcher's

    Write (a), (b), (c) or (d) in the box.

6. Barbecues were not allowed.

    True ☐   False ☐

★ ★ ★

7. Tick the activities mentioned:

    Table tennis ☐

    Treasure–hunt ☐

    Swimming ☐

★ ★ ★

8. Who played in the football match? ....

9. How many bicycles did they hire? ....

10. What did they go to visit? ....

30. Le bulletin météo

You will hear a weather forecast for each of the days of an entire week.

Fill in the details in the grid, giving two items for each day:

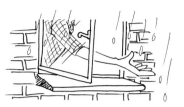

Monday	(i)
	(ii)
Tuesday	(i)
	(ii)
Wednesday	(i)
	(ii)
Thursday	(i)
	(ii)
Friday	(i)
	(ii)
Saturday	(i)
	(ii)
Sunday	(i)
	(ii)

31. Les informations

You will hear two news items and a weather forecast.

1. First news item

1. When did this incident take place? ....

2. How many young people were involved? ....

3. What did they decide to do? ....

   ....

★   ★   ★

4. Their boat hit

   (a) a sandbank

   (b) a ship

   (c) a rock

   (d) another boat

   Write (a), (b), (c) or (d) in the box.

5. How did they attract attention to their situation? ....

   ....

6. How long were they waiting to be rescued? ....

★   ★   ★

2. Second news item

1. Where did this hunting accident take place? ....

2. What age was the man? ....

3. He had left home to go shooting

   (a) deer

   (b) foxes

   (c) rabbits

   (d) pheasants

   Write (a), (b), (c) or (d) in the box.

4. He accidentally shot himself in

   (a) the face

   (b) the arm

   (c) the chest

   (d) the leg

   Write (a), (b), (c) or (d) in the box.

★　★　★

5. Who called the ambulance? ....

6. When did the man die? ....

★　★　★

3. Weather forecast

1. Fill in the weather details in the grid:

Morning	(i)
	(ii)
Afternoon	(i)
	(ii)

2. What should you remember to bring if you are going out?

   ....

32. Infos sportives

You will hear news about three major sports events.

1. Formula 1 racing

1. When did Michael Shumacher win his sixth world title?...........................

★   ★   ★

2. Write down three of the qualities which make him a great champion.

    (i)..

    (ii)...

    (iii)..

★   ★   ★

2. Rugby

1. Fill in the result in the grid:

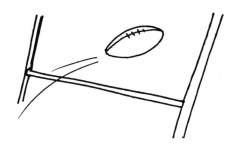

Scotland	
Japan	

★   ★   ★

2. Who are Scotland's next opponents?..

3. When will this match take place? ....

★   ★   ★

3. Tennis

1. What nationality was the winner? ....

2. What nationality was the loser? ....

3. Write down the score in the second and third sets:

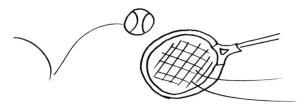

First set	7–5
Second set	
Third set	

33. Mon petit boulot

Nathalie tells us about her part-time job.

1. What age is Nathalie? ....

2. When did she find this job in the restaurant?..................................

3. Why would she not like to continue working as a waitress later on in life?

    ....

★   ★   ★

4. How far from the restaurant does she live? ....

5. At what time in the morning does she start work? ....

6. At what time does the evening part of her work begin?..................

★   ★   ★

7. What does her work consist of? *(two details)*

    (i)...

    (ii)..

8. What is pleasant about her job?..

★   ★   ★

9. What part of the job does she not like? ....

10. What makes up for the salary which, she says, isn't good? ....

un petit boulot
un horaire
on a quelques
heures de repos
débarrasser
les tables

49

34. Mes impressions sur l'Irlande

Two young French people have spent a while in Ireland. They tell us about their experiences.

1. Nicole

1. When did Nicole come to Ireland? ....

2. Who accompanied her? ....

3. How long did she spend here?

    (a) A few days

    (b) A week

    (c) A fortnight

    (d) A month

    Write (a), (b), (c) or (d) in the box.

4. What was her favourite part of the country? ....

5. She really liked the beaches and the sheep.

    True ☐   False ☐

    ★   ★   ★

6. What does she say about the town of Dingle? *(two details)*

    (i)..

    (ii)..

7. As a souvenir, she bought a silver pendant, a dolphin.

    True ☐   False ☐

    ★   ★   ★

50

2. André

1. In which month did André come to Ireland?...

2. How long did he spend here?...

3. In which French city does André live?..

4. When will the Irish students go to France on the second leg of the exchange? ....

★   ★   ★

5. What did he like about his holiday here?...

6. Mention two sports activities in which he took part:

   (i)...

   (ii)..

35. Où sont-ils ?

Conversations are taking place in different locations.

1. First conversation

1. What colour trousers does the lady buy? ....

2. She also buys a blouse but decides not to buy a skirt.

    True ☐   False ☐

3. Fill in the details in the grid:

Cost of trousers	€
Cost of blouse	€
Total cost	€

4. How does the lady pay for the items? ....

★   ★   ★

2. Second conversation

1. The person is suffering from

    (a) a toothache

    (b) a sore throat

    (c) a headache

    (d) an earache

    Write (a), (b), (c) or (d) in the box.   ☐

2. How often per day should he take the tablets? ....

3. How much does he pay? ....

★   ★   ★

3. Third conversation

1. Fill in the details in the grid:

Number of tickets bought	
Girl's age	
Grandmother's age	
Cost of grandmother's ticket	
Length of video	

2. They are visiting

   (a) a museum

   (b) a castle

   (c) an art gallery

   (d) a factory

   Write (a), (b), (c) or (d) in the box.

36. Au restaurant

Monsieur and Madame Dupré are dining in a restaurant.

1. For what time has Monsieur Dupré made the reservation?

    ....

2. Where is the restaurant situated? ....

3. Why has Monsieur Dupré chosen this restaurant?

    ....

★   ★   ★

4. Where does Monsieur Dupré ask to be seated?

    ....

5. How long will they have to wait to get their choice of table?

    ....

6. What does the manager suggest they might do while waiting?

    ....

★   ★   ★

7. Fill in the details about their meal:

	Monsieur Dupré	Madame Dupré
Starter		
Main course		

8. What do they choose to drink? ....

37. Mes vacances préférées

People are talking about their holidays.

1. Eric and Anne

1. Where does Anne spend Christmas day? ....

2. In total, how many people will be there?

 (a) 3

 (b) 4

 (c) 5

 (d) 6

 Write (a), (b), (c) or (d) in the box.

2. Céline and Joseph

1. In which month does Joseph like to go on holidays? ....

2. Where does the family go to ski? ....

3. Where does the family stay? ....

4. What does the grandmother like to do? ....

★   ★   ★

3. Jean and Thérèse

1. Thérèse prefers the summer holidays to the Easter holidays.

 True ☐ False ☐

2. What form of transport do Thérèse and her parents use? ....

3. What do they like to visit? *(two details)*

 (i) ....

 (ii) ....

4. What kind of holidays does Jean prefer? ....

38. Trois petites annonces

You will hear three advertisements.

1. First advertisement

Fill in the details about the missing cat:

Name of cat (in French)	
Age	
Colour	
Colour of one ear	
Length of whiskers	

★ ★ ★

2. Second advertisement

1. What language should the penpal speak? ....

2. What interests should he/she have? *(three details)*

    (i)..

    (ii)...

    (iii)..

3. What is the name of the person who has placed the advertisement?

    ....

4. How should he/she be contacted?..

★ ★ ★

3. Third advertisement

Fill in the details of what the girl has lost:

Day	
Date	
Place	
Item lost	
Telephone number	*03 10 21 86 _ _*

39. Les accidents de la route

You will hear details of three road accidents.

1. First accident

1. How long did the driver have his licence? ....

2. Fill in the details about the accident:

City	
Age of driver	
Time of accident	
Type of vehicle	
Number of passengers	
Injuries to passengers	

★   ★   ★

2. Second accident

1. What age was Pierre Lafitte? ....

2. Why did the accident occur? *(two details)*

    (i) ....

    (ii) ....

3. What was Pierre doing when he was knocked down? ....

4. In which city was the hospital? ....

5. Pierre was injured

    (a) on the arms

    (b) on the legs

    (c) on the head

    (d) on the shoulders

    Write (a), (b), (c) or (d) in the box.

★   ★   ★

58

3. Third accident

1. What age was Dominque Mathieu? ....

2. With whom was she cycling? ....

3. In which city was the hospital? ....

4. Where was she injured? ....

5. What did the driver of the car not have? ....

40. Visite au musée

Philippe has brought his family to visit the museum.

1. Fill in the details about the tickets:

Number of tickets	
Ages of children	
Cost of family ticket	€

★　★　★

2. At what time does the museum close in the evening? ....

3. On which day does the museum not open? ....

4. Where is the restaurant situated?

    ....

41. Les sorties

People are talking about going out.

1. Odile and Pierre

1. What has Odile won? ....

2. What type of film is it? ....

3. At what time does the film begin? ....

4. Where will they meet? ....

5. At what time will they meet? ....

★   ★   ★

2. Henri and Caroline

1. When did Henri go to the theatre? ....

2. What does Caroline prefer? ....

3. How many actors were in the play? ....

4. Why does Henri not like the cinema? ....

42. On fait des réservations

People are making reservations for holiday accommodation.

1. Campsite

Fill in the details in the grid:

Number of tents	
Number of adults	
Number of children	
Number of nights they will stay	
Dates that they will stay	

★   ★   ★

2. Hotel

1. For how many people is this booking being made? ....

2. Why is the hotel almost booked out this evening? ....

3. Fill in the details in the grid:

Floor	
Number of rooms	
Price	€

★   ★   ★

3. Youth hostel

Fill in the details in this form:

Number of people	
Dates of the stay	
Dormitories or private rooms?	
Name	*Figère*
Credit card number	*2 3 4 5 8 6 6 9 7 0*
Expiry date of card	
Address	

43. De quelle région viens-tu ?

Three people talk about the region in which they live.

1. Marie

1. What is Marie's region?...

2. Which sports do people practise here? *(three details)*

    (i)...

    (ii)...

    (iii)...

3. Why do people come to the region in the summer? *(two details)*

    (i) ....

    (ii) ....

★ ★ ★

2. Paul

1. What is grown in the Languedoc-Roussillon region?

    ....

2. Write down the name of three countries from which tourists come in the summer.

    (i)...

    (ii)...

    (iii)...

3. For what two reasons do tourists come here?

    (i)...

    (ii)...

★ ★ ★

3. Cécile

1. In which region does Cécile live? ....

2. Write down two similarities between the region and Ireland.

    (i)..

    (ii)..

3. Why is the weather very like that in Ireland?

    ....

4. Which two comic-strip characters are associated with the region?

    (i)..

    (ii)..

44. Ce que je préfère

Three people talk to us about their personal preferences.

1. Janine

1. What colour does Janine like? ....

2. Where, according to Janine, can this colour be seen? *(three details)*

    (i)..

    (ii)...

    (iii)..

★   ★   ★

2. Jean

1. Jean loves *gratin dauphinois*. With which ingredients is it made? *(three details)*

    (i)..

    (ii)...

    (iii)..

2. Who prepares it for him? ....

3. On what special occasion does he like to eat it?................................

★   ★   ★

3. Sophie

1. Why does Sophie like art?...

2. When she was young, what did she like to draw? *(three details)*

    (i)..

    (ii)...

    (iii)..

3. Her teacher gives her useful information about this difficult subject.

    True ☐   False ☐

45. Deux présentations

Two young people describe themselves.

Fill in the details in the grids:

1.

Name	*Virginie*
Colour of hair	
Colour of eyes	
Older sister's age	
Younger sister's age	
Hobbies	
Mother's job	
Father's job	
Career ambition	
Favourite sports	

★   ★   ★

2.

Name	*Etienne*
Colour of eyes	
Colour of hair	
Age	
Date of birthday	
Father's job	
Summer activity	
Brother's age	
Brother's hobby	
Mother's job	

46. On parle des vacances

Listen to two conversations in which people are making plans for their holidays.

1. Mother and Father

1. What decision has the mother made? ....

2. What items will they hire out? *(four details)*

   (i)..

   (ii)...

   (iii)..

   (iv)..

3. What three items will they buy?

   (i)..

   (ii)...

   (iii)..

4. Where does Mother think they should go on holiday for the children's sake? ....

5. On what day of the week does this conversation take place?....................

★   ★   ★

2. Sophie and Paul

1. This conversation takes place

   (a) during the summer

   (b) before Christmas

   (c) after Christmas

   (d) at Easter

   Write (a), (b), (c) or (d) in the box.

2. Where would Sophie like to rent a villa?...

3. In which month would she like to go on holidays?

   ....

4. Describe the villa that she has seen in the brochures. *(four details)*

   (i)...

   (ii)..

   (iii)...

   (iv)...

5. How far from the beach is the villa situated? ....

47. A l'aéroport

Three people are making enquiries about their flight at the airport.

1. First passenger
Fill in the details in the grid:

City to which he is travelling	
Name of the airline	
Scheduled time of departure	
Number of hours of flight delay	
Cause of the delay	

★   ★   ★

2. Second passenger

1. What is the young lady asked to produce? *(two details)*

    (i)...

    (ii)..

2. How many items of luggage does she have?

    (a) 2

    (b) 3

    (c) 4

    (d) 5

    Write (a), (b), (c) or (d) in the box.

3. How many kilos does her luggage weigh? ....

4. How much does she have to pay for having excess luggage? ....

★   ★   ★

3. Third passenger

Fill in the details in the grid:

Flight number	
City of destination	
Time of departure	
Gate number	

48. Bon voyage à tous !

**Listen to three tempting
holiday offers.**

1. First advertisement

Fill in the details in the grid:

Length of holiday on offer	
Where in France?	
Type of accommodation	
Price per person	

★   ★   ★

2. Second advertisement

1. What would you be doing if you went on this holiday?.............................

2. Where in France would you be? ....

3. For how long would you be there?..

4. How much would this holiday cost?..

★   ★   ★

3. Third advertisement

1. What would do you good?..

2. What choice of accommodation would you have?

    ....

3. How much does this holiday cost?

    (i) High season: € _____

    (ii) Low season: € _____

49. Des cadeaux

People are discussing presents for special occasions.

1. Luc and Marie

1. When is Mother's Day?...

2. What present has Marie bought for her mother? ....

3. How long has Marie's mother been going to art classes?....................

★　★　★

2. Sophie and Paul

1. When is Father's Day?...

2. What item does Sophie suggest Paul could buy?..............................

3. What three colours does she mention?

    (i)...

    (ii)..

    (iii)...

4. What does Paul decide to buy for his father?...................................

★　★　★

3. Janine and Aurélie

1. What is the date of Aurélie's sister's birthday? ....

2. In town, Aurélie saw

    (a) a beautiful ring

    (b) a lovely bag

    (c) a silver watch

    (d) a rare coin

    Write (a), (b), (c) or (d) in the box.

73

50. Visite d'une ville

Jean–Marc and his wife are on holiday in a French town. They want to explore the town by bicycle.

1. Fill in the details in the grid:

Day of proposed tour	
Date	
Names of the two cyclists	*Jean-Marc and*
Name of their hotel	
Starting time of tour	
Meeting place	

★   ★   ★

2. Fill in the details in the grid:

Two prices for the tour	(i)	(ii)
What is included in the lower price?	(i) (ii)	
Advice given at the end		

51. Les téléphones portables : on parle de deux incidents

Mobile phones are useful, but they can sometimes cause problems! Listen to two conversations.

1. Thérèse and Alice

1. Who is in hospital? ....
2. Since when has he been there? ....
3. What happened to him? ....
4. Where did the accident happen? ....
5. What is his injury? ....

★   ★   ★

2. Jean and David

1. When did David get his mobile phone? ....
2. Who gave it to him? ....
3. During which class did his mobile phone ring? ....
4. When did this happen? ....
5. What happened the next day in school? ....

52. Les informations

You will hear two news items and a weather forecast.

1. First news item

1. When did these floods take place? ....

2. Which river has burst its banks? ....

3. The firemen have brought people
   (a) to the town hall
   (b) to the fire station
   (c) to a hotel
   (d) to the railway station
   Write (a), (b), (c) or (d) in the box.

4. On which two days will schools remain closed?

   (i) ....

   (ii) ....

5. What are the final two digits in the telephone number?

0	5	2	2	6	6	0	7	_	_

★ ★ ★

2. Second news item

1. Where have these fires occurred? ....

2. How many villages have been cut off by the flames? ....

3. A fireman has been burned on the
   (a) hand
   (b) arm
   (c) face
   (d) leg
   Write (a), (b), (c) or (d) in the box.

4. Why is the second fireman in hospital? ....

★ ★ ★

3. Weather forecast

Fill in the weather details in the grid:

North	(i)	
	(ii)	
Centre	(i)	
	(ii)	
South	(i)	
	(ii)	

La Moitié Nord

La Moitié Sud

53. On dîne au restaurant

Monsieur and Madame Legrand are dining in a restaurant.

1. The couple who have almost finished their meal are sitting

    (a) near the window

    (b) near the door

    (c) near the kitchen

    (d) near the fireplace

    Write (a), (b), (c) or (d) in the box.

2. What do Monsieur and Madame Legrand do while waiting for a table?

    ....

3. The manager of the restaurant gives them the fixed-price menu and the wine list.

    True ☐   False ☐

    ★   ★   ★

4. Madame Legrand would like some ice in her *apéritif*.

    True ☐   False ☐

    ★   ★   ★

5. Fill in the details of what they order:

	Monsieur Legrand	Madame Legrand
Starter		
Main course		
Dessert		

6. What do they choose to drink? ....

7. The total cost comes to €33.

    True ☐   False ☐

54. Des accidents de la route

People are discussing road accidents.

1. Luc and Claire

1. Where does Luc say that the accident took place?

   ....

2. A Peugeot car collided with

   (a) another car

   (b) a cyclist

   (c) a horse

   (d) a pedestrian

   Write (a), (b), (c) or (d) in the box.

3. How many people were injured?...

4. A truck and a van were also involved in the collision.

   True ☐   False ☐

★   ★   ★

2. A son and his mother

1. When did the accident occur?...

2. What two vehicles were involved?...

   (i)...

   (ii)...

3. What was the cause of the accident?...

4. What age was the young man? ....

5. The young man was unconscious when he was taken to hospital.

   True ☐   False ☐

55. Au poste de police

People call to the police station to report the loss or theft of an item.

1. First caller

1. Was the item lost or stolen?...

2. What was the item? ....

3. Where was the person? ....

★   ★   ★

2. Second caller
Fill in the details in the grid:

Lost or stolen?	
What was the item?	
Where did this happen?	
Description of item	

★   ★   ★

3. Third caller

1. What has been stolen?..............................

2. Where was the person? ....

3. Describe the thief. *(two details)*

    (i)..

    (ii)...

4. Fill in the details:

Contents	(i)
	(ii)
	(iii)

56. La météo pour les quatre saisons en France

You will hear four weather forecasts, one for each season.

1. Spring
Fill in the weather details in the grid:

Temperatures expected	
Weather for most of France	
Weather in the south	
Weather in the north	

★   ★   ★

2. Summer

1. What will the temperature be in Provence?..........................

2. Who, in particular, should be careful?...

3. During what hours is the use of sun-cream recommended?

    ....

★   ★   ★

3. Autumn
Fill in the weather details in the grid:

North of France	(i)
	(ii)
South of France	
Weather in afternoon	(i)
	(ii)

★   ★   ★

81

4. Winter

1. Above what altitude in the mountains will it snow?......................................

2. What are the predictions for the daytime? *(two details)*

   (i)..

   (ii)..

3. When should one be careful on the roads? ....

57. Le travail

Two people talk about their jobs.

1. A nurse

1. Why does she like her job? ....

2. Why are people in a bad humour from time to time? ....

    ....

3. Why does she prefer working during the day?

    ....

★   ★   ★

2. A mechanic

1. How far from his home is the garage? ....

2. There is a good atmosphere at work

    (a) because people chat and joke a lot

    (b) because everyone likes the work

    (c) because the boss is friendly

    (d) because all the mechanics are young

    Write (a), (b), (c) or (d) in the box.

3. What age was he when he bought his first moped? ....

4. When it's not raining, how does he travel to work? ....

58. Quelle surprise !

Thérèse's mother loves doing competitions.

1. Where does Thérèse's mother find the competitions? ....

2. On which day did she get an important telephone call?............................

3. What was she told to do? ....

★   ★   ★

4. For how many weeks will she be going on holidays? ....

5. To which country will she be going? ....

6. Why is Thérèse delighted too?

....

59. Quel est mon métier ?

Three people describe their occupations.

Guess the occupation of these three people.

	Occupation
1.	
2.	
3.	

60. Des invités

Guests are arriving. Listen to three conversations.

1. Marie and her grandmother

1. How long has it been since Marie saw her grandparents?..........................

2. The first train

   (a) was crowded

   (b) arrived late

   (c) arrived on time

   (d) was nicer than the second one

   Write (a), (b), (c) or (d) in the box.

★   ★   ★

2. Thomas and Janine

1. Why was the journey difficult for Thomas? *(two details)*

   (i)..

   (ii)...

2. What had Janine heard on the radio?...

3. What did Janine offer Thomas as a choice of drink? *(three details)*

   (i) ....

   (ii)...

   (iii)..

4. What drink did Thomas ask for? ....

★   ★   ★

3. Juliette and Lydie

1. For how long can Juliette come to Lydie's house?..........................

2. When can she come? ....

3. What is the date of Lydie's birthday? ....

4. Fill in the details in the grid:

Departure time of train	
Arrival time of train	
City of destination	

61. Au restaurant

People are dining in a restaurant. Listen to two conversations.

1. A waiter and Madame Blanchaud

1. For how many people has Madame Blanchaud reserved a table? ....

2. Where is their table situated?...

3. What is written on the board? *(two details)*

    (i)...

    (ii)..

4. What will they drink?...

★ ★ ★

2. A waiter and Monsieur Duhamel

1. Fill in the details of what Monsieur Duhamel orders:

Food	Drinks
(i)	(i)
(ii)	(ii)
(iii)	(iii)

2. He asks for sugar, paper napkins and

    (a) a small plate

    (b) a little spoon

    (c) a little knife

    (d) a small fork

    Write (a), (b), (c) or (d) in the box.

62. La publicité

Listen to three advertisements.

1. First advertisement

1. What three varieties of fish are mentioned?

    (i)..

    (ii)...

    (iii)..

2. Why, according to the advertisement, should you eat fresh fish?

    ....

★   ★   ★

2. Second advertisement

1. What is the advantage of having Canal +?

    ....

2. What is the special offer? ....

3. Until what date is the special offer available? ....

★   ★   ★

3. Third advertisement

1. Which of the four seasons is mentioned?...

2. You can get a return ticket to Madrid or Rome for €50.

    True ☐   False ☐

3. Where can you get a ticket? *(two details)*

    (i)..

    (ii)...

63. Bonne chance !

It's National Lottery day! Caroline may be lucky!

1. Fill in the details in the grid:

Day	
Date	
Number of scratch cards bought	
Total cost of scratch cards	
Number of Lotto tickets bought	
Total amount paid	

★　★　★

2. At what time was the Lotto draw?..

3. There were six winning numbers.
    Fill in the missing ones:

2		12		24	

4. How many of the winning numbers did Caroline have? ....

64. Petites annonces

Listen to four advertisements.

1. First advertisement

1. What does Catherine Morel collect? ....

2. In which French city does she live? ....

★ ★ ★

2. Second advertisement

1. What is Paul Legrand looking for? ....

2. On what condition would he pay a good price?

....

3. When should Paul Legrand be contacted? ....

★ ★ ★

3. Third advertisement

1. What items should you not throw away? *(two details)*

   (i) ....

   (ii) ....

2. What should you do with them instead?

....

★ ★ ★

4. Fourth advertisement

1. Whom would this person like to contact? *(two details)*

   (i) ....

   (ii) ....

2. When should you contact him? ....

65. Mon émission de télévision préférée

Two young people talk about their favourite television programme.

1. Maude

1. How many television sets does her family have? ....

2. What is the name of her favourite programme?...

3. How many young people feature in the programme? ....

4. How long do the participants spend in the house?...................................

★ ★ ★

2. Yannick

1. What is Yannick's favourite sport?...

2. On what is his favourite programme based? ....

★ ★ ★

3. When does he watch the programme? ....

4. Why does Yannick find the programme interesting?

    ....

66. En réclame !

Certain items are going cheap!

1. First advertisement

1. Write down three of the camping equipment items.

   (i)..

   (ii)...

   (iii)..

2. Write the missing digits in the telephone number:

0	4	3	3	_	_	0	6	_	_

3. When should you phone? ....

★   ★   ★

2. Second advertisement

1. Write down the list of dairy products:

Dairy products	
(i)	
(ii)	
(iii)	
(iv)	
(v)	

2. On which items is there a 20% reduction?

   (i)..

   (ii)...

★   ★   ★

3. Third advertisement

1. What is being sold? ....

2. What is the price? ....

3. What is included in the price? ....

4. When should you phone? ....

4. Fourth advertisement

1. Describe the cat that you could adopt. *(two details)*

   (i) ....

   (ii) ....

2. What age is it? ....

3. How much would it cost to phone the number given? ....

67. Des recettes de cuisine

Two young people have returned from their travels with interesting recipes.

1. Aurélie

1. From which country has Aurélie returned? ....

2. For how many people is the recipe? ....

3. How many tomatoes do you need? ....

4. How many slices of ham do you need?..

★   ★   ★

5. Write down two of the instructions.

   (i)...

   (ii)..

★   ★   ★

2. Antoine

1. When was Antoine in Ireland? ....

2. Of what does he still dream? ....

3. How many eggs do you need? ....

4. The tomato should be ripe.

   True ☐   False ☐

5. You need a few mushrooms and two slices of black pudding.

   True ☐   False ☐

★   ★   ★

6. Which of the ingredients should you not put on the pan? ....

7. With what should you serve this meal? *(two details)*

   (i)...

   (ii)..

95

68. Silence, on tourne !

Caroline tells Philippe about an interesting job that she has.

1. Where is Caroline going?...

2. When is the filming going to begin? ....

3. Where will the programme be set?...

4. What age should young people be if they would like to take part?.............

★   ★   ★

5. How much is one paid? ....

6. At what time does filming stop?..

69. Horoscope du mois

Count your lucky stars! Listen to a selection of horoscope predictions.

Fill in the details in the grids:

1. Aries

Dates	
One piece of advice given	
Lucky colour	
Lucky number	

★ ★ ★

2. Leo

Dates	
One piece of advice given	
Lucky colour	
Lucky number	

★ ★ ★

3. Libra

Dates	
One piece of advice given	
Lucky colour	
Lucky number	

★ ★ ★

4. Taurus

Dates	
One piece of advice given	
Lucky colour	
Lucky number	

70. Pour aller à ... ?

People are looking for directions.

1. First person

1. Where does the man want to go?..

2. What directions are given to him? *(three details)*

   (i)..

   (ii)...

   (iii)..

3. How far away is it?...

★   ★   ★

2. Second person

1. Where does the lady want to go? ....

2. Cross the bridge and take the first street on the right.

   True ☐   False ☐

3. How far away is it?...

★   ★   ★

3. Third person

1. Where does the man want to go?...

2. Turn right, and take the first street on the left.

   True ☐   False ☐

3. How far away is it?...

4. Fourth person

1. What is the lady looking for? ....

2. What directions should she follow? *(two details)*

   (i)...

   (ii)..

3. How long will it take her to get there?

   ....